THAT'S WHAT I THOUGHT

ABOUT THE
LEXI RUDNITSKY EDITOR'S CHOICE AWARD

The Lexi Rudnitsky Editor's Choice Award is given annually to a poetry collection by a writer who has published at least once previous book of poems. Along with the Lexi Rudnitsky First Book Prize in Poetry, it is a collaboration of Persea Books and the Lexi Rudnitsky Poetry Project. Entry guidelines for both awards are available on Persea's website (www. perseabooks.com).

Lexi Rudnitsky (1972–2005) grew up outside of Boston, and studied at Brown University and Columbia University. Her own poems exhibit both a playful love of language and a fierce conscience. Her writing appeared in *The Antioch Review, Columbia: A Journal of Literature and Art, The Nation, The New Yorker, The Paris Review, Pequod*, and *The Western Humanities Review*. In 2004, she won the Milton Kessler Memorial Prize for Poetry from *Harpur Palate*.

Lexi died suddenly in 2005, just months after the birth of her first child and the acceptance for publication of her first book of poems, *A Doorless Knocking into Night* (Mid-List Press, 2006). The Lexi Rudnitsky book prizes were created to memorialize her by promoting the type of poet and poetry in which she so spiritedly believed.

Previous winners of the Lexi Rudnitsky Editor's Choice Award:

2016 Heather Derr-Smith, *Thrust*
2015 Shane McCrae, *The Animal Too Big to Kill*
2014 Caki Wilkinson, *The Wynona Stone Poems*
2013 Michael White, *Vermeer in Hell*
2012 Mitchell L. H. Douglas, *blak al-fə bet*
2011 Amy Newman, *Dear Editor*

THAT'S WHAT I THOUGHT

POEMS

GARY YOUNG

A Karen & Michael Braziller Book

PERSEA BOOKS / NEW YORK

Persea Books, Inc.
277 Broadway
New York, New York 1007

Library of Congress Cataloging-in-Publication Data

Names: Young, Gary, 1951– author.
Title: That's what I thought : poems / Gary Young.
Other titles: That is what I thought
Description: New York : Persea Books, 2018. | "A Karen & Michael Braziller Book."
Identifiers: LCCN 2018017954 | ISBN 9780892554942 (original trade pbk. : alk= . paper)
Classification: LCC PS3575.O785 A6 2018 | DDC 811/.54—dc23
LC record available at https://lccn.loc.gov/2018017954

Book design and composition by Rita Lascaro
Typeset in Stone Serif
Manufactured in the United States of America. Printed on acid-free paper.

for Gene Holtan, 1930–2016

CONTENTS

O the mind, mind has mountains...

—GERARD MANLEY HOPKINS

All that's left of the fabled residence is a teahouse on a tiny island in the center of a pond. The great hall must have been beautiful; the little house and the bridge beside it are lovely even now. Wisteria sways along a trellis that rises from the pond, and three turtles rest on a rock beside a slender crane. The water is marked with the dark shadows of cedar and pine, and enormous carp circle the pond endlessly, without knowing they're in a pond, without knowing that they're carp.

In the woods, hunting mushrooms, I saw a flash of white, and thought Amanita, Death Cap, but it was just a piece of paper. When I picked it up, I recognized my own handwriting. It was a note I must have written months before and dropped. Waterlogged and half-eaten by slugs, the ink was faded, but I could read, *the willingness to use our minds is what erodes our minds.*

Five ravens climbed a redwood, hopping from one limb to another. They could have flown to the top of the tree, but they took their time, and stopped to preen before jumping to the next branch. The woodpeckers, who'd hectored the ravens all morning, sat in another tree and watched the ravens as they made their slow ascent. It's difficult to be honest with yourself; that's why it's good to have an adversary.

In a shack outside Oaxaca, a shirtless man in torn pants offered to sell me his father's bones. He unfolded a filthy handkerchief that cradled dirt clods and a few broken twigs. He held them as he might have held a small bird, put them to his lips, and whispered something I couldn't hear. He raised them to his ear, nodded, and brought them to his lips again. He spread the handkerchief on the table, lowered his head, and said, no. He folded the dirty cloth, and stumbled out the door whispering, no, no.

As usual, the birds wake me with their racket at first light. The water in the rice field is iridescent beneath the slender green slips. Bamboo and pine trees blanket the hills beyond. I recognize the cooing dove, the sparrow and the thrush. How did they find me here, on the other side of the world?

We grew up hearing war stories. The man next door came to beside his downed plane, and discovered someone cutting off his finger for his ring. In the backyard, we shot the pistol he'd taken from an Italian officer. My father hunted men in the caves of Okinawa. His friend found the skull of a Japanese soldier there, polished it to a bright sheen, and sent it home to his father. Down the block, a neighbor gave his son a handful of photographs—women playing with their breasts, a man entering a woman from behind, a group of soldiers standing in a circle around someone with a sword. Such extravagant, incomprehensible gifts: the women, the gun, a man kneeling beside his own head, which had fallen a short distance from his body.

On Sunday afternoons, my grandmother and I rode a little rail car called Angel's Flight from Third Street up to the Olive Street station. At the top of the run, she told me about angels—this was the City of Angels—and about the heavenly host poised somewhere above the clouds. Driving home, we passed three white crosses planted on a hillside overlooking the highway. She told me about the crucifixion, and I came to believe that Jesus and the others had been crucified on those very crosses. I was never happy living in that city, where terrible things had happened.

Last night's rain stripped every leaf from the Japanese maple, and this morning, the tree seems to float above a pool of gold. Clouds, knotted and ropy against the blue, are visible now through the barren limbs, and a single monarch, early arrival or late to leave, stutters on the damp, unstable air.

As a guide described the origins of the Phoenix Hall, discussed the intricate carvings, and explained the symbolism of the lotus, an old man stood at the railing before the enormous Buddha there, and prayed. He held the photograph of a young woman to his chest, the girl's face directed outward, toward the statue. His lips barely moved as he mumbled his prayer. The guide led her group out of the chamber, and when it was just the two of us, the old man turned the photograph toward me and continued to pray. We walked together out of the hall, while behind us, bodhisattvas sailed around the room on clouds, some ringing cymbals or beating drums, all of them so mesmerized by the sight of the Pure Land, they seemed to pay no attention as we walked away.

The boy rode his bike to the artist's studio every day after school to watch him paint. Sometimes there was a nude sitting in the middle of the room, and the boy studied her quietly from a chair in the corner. Years later, he bought several paintings from the old man, and remembering those days lost in the model's flesh, asked to buy one of his nudes. There aren't any, the old man said. I've never painted a nude. But the model, he said. Oh, she was just there to look at.

We climbed the mountain, looking for the mountain, unsure of what we'd find. Cicadas hummed in the moist air, and two ravens called out as they circled overhead. Sunset lit the far side of the summit. A stand of bamboo swayed above us, making the mountain appear to breathe, and we kept walking, the mountain alive beneath our feet.

One day past the solstice, trees obscured by mist, today shorter than yesterday, tomorrow shorter than today, gnats are in a frenzy above the hollyhocks, woodpeckers pound at the redwood's dusty bark, and new fruit swells on the persimmon tree.

At dusk, a whale surfaced in the cove, close to shore. His body was black, but his breath was white, vaporous, and ghostly. Even after nightfall, I could sense his body floating there. If I rest my head against the darkness, I can hear its heartbeat. It sounds like a cricket calling outside my window.

Beach grass caught the milky froth blown in from the sea. There were footprints above the tide line, but the sand was smooth where the ocean had retreated. My sons were sleeping beside me at the water's edge. If I'd wakened them, they would have seen a crow, a fish rolling in the shallow surf, and two dogs loping along the shore, nipping at one another's ankles as they ran.

I can't remember everything. I can't remember the name of Vic
Silver's wife, though I recall the number tattooed on her arm,
the iron fence around their house, the grates on their windows,
the alarms, and the gems hoarded in their basement. Every
morning, Vic Silver lit a cigar, let it go out, and chewed what
was left all day. He carried a wad of bills as thick as my wrist,
and he'd peel off hundreds for a car or a necklace. He sold my
mother jewelry at a bargain. My wife sometimes wears the ring
I bought from him when I was a boy. Every afternoon on my
walk home from school, I picked a pomegranate from the tree
that grew beside his shop. The plant was so laden with fruit,
I didn't think he'd notice.

A robin calls out from the redwoods. Siskins chatter at the feeder, and doves coo side-by-side on the roof. An eagle drifts overhead, shrieking like a lost child. A house finch runs his scales, and a chickadee repeats—*chickadee, chickadee.* How strange. My father, who could not imagine a world in which he didn't exist, is dead, and the birds keep singing.

Driving from the valley to my home in the mountains, I saw persimmons and pomegranates bend spindly boughs almost to the ground. In every direction there were trees marking each farm with a pattern distinct as a fingerprint—date palms, blue spruce, walnut, cypress, olive and sycamore surrounding, protecting and dwarfing a farmhouse and barn. There were rows of peach trees, their trunks swollen over the grafted rootstock, and grape vines thick as my thigh. Every hundred feet an owl box sat perched on a pole. Dust rose behind a tractor, billowed and trailed away in a pattern identical to the clouds that stretched across the sky. Cotton bolls gleaned from the fields by a persistent wind dotted fences and the thorny weeds by the side of the road. The cemeteries were filled with flowers, as if a feast were taking place, a party, a wedding. Almost home, I glimpsed the fluorescent rust of a Dawn Redwood about to drop its leaves. I'd driven past that tree a hundred times before, and never noticed it.

Repeated beneath the surface of the pond, the redwoods reach impossible depths, and below them, clouds gather and pass on. Fish slip in and out of the branches of the trees, immortal carp drifting through the chill, inexhaustible bowl of heaven.

It was five o'clock, and the clock in the old stone tower rang five times. The narrow streets were already in shadow, but light still played over the rafters and the red tile roofs. We could smell the sea on the warm air that billowed the sheets drying on the balconies. A cloud of gnats rose and fell on the breeze, and swallows appeared from their nests hidden under the cornice of the buildings. They spun and darted overhead, harvesting the sky.

From a knoll above the house, I can see deep into the canyon. Sunlight has made its way through the tangle of redwood and tanoak, and here and there, set fire to the trembling shadows.

At sixty, I've made progress eliminating anger from my heart, and ridding myself of attachment to things. I have freed my mind of troubling thoughts and foolish distractions, but I cannot seem to cure myself of lust. I suffer every affection—pleasant colors, smooth skin, soothing voices. To tame these passions, a sutra suggests that we meditate on the body's impurities—feces, urine, smeared blood, scorched bones—or imagine being devoured by wild animals. I have tried. It may well be that a living body is like a rotten corpse, neither one worthy of desire, but how could I ever turn away from my son's dark eyes or the music of my boy's sweet voice when he calls to me?

The sky grew dark, and mosquitos danced above the surface of the stream. A small trout hovered in place above the gravel bed, then flew from the water, and plucked the insects from the air again and again.

Gathering mushrooms in the forest, I saw a mountain lion slip behind a tree and move off toward the stream. The sun was setting, and light streamed up the canyon and lit the tops of the redwoods. I found one last mushroom at the base of a rotted stump, and carried it out of the shadows and into the meadow, where persimmons were shining on their slender branches, and the leaves of the wisteria whirled in the air as they fell from the upper reaches of the vine.

After the solstice, the days were getting longer, but not long enough. Another storm was building over the ocean. In the distance, there were perforations in the darkness, a fugitive swarm of shearwaters that turned as one, the feathers beneath their wings flashing white above the ocean that roiled against the unyielding cliffs.

14,000 years ago, in the mountains above Nara, a ravine was filled with boulders to match the constellations overhead—to conjure the Milky Way, and to mirror a river of stars with a river of stones. When I knelt there, I could hear the faint murmur of water far below, the same soft whisper we hear at night, when we look up at the stars.

The whale's tooth was etched with a needle or a fine blade to pass the time on a long voyage. On one side, a woman sits bare-chested, a cloth draped over her lap, her body disproportioned, the execution awkward. On the other, a three-masted whaler in full sail is depicted in stunning detail, the proportions perfect, the masts and rigging rendered with passion and precision. The sailor had seen more ships than naked women, or perhaps his drawings betrayed his truest affections. The woman was a gauzy memory, an invention, but the ship was at hand.

The fire grew larger every day, an enormous arrow of flame pointed at our house. For three days I hiked through the woods to avoid roadblocks, and watered the garden and my trees. The air was tinted yellow by the smoke, and even things close at hand seemed far away. The few birds that remained sang songs I didn't recognize, songs I'd never heard. Our house was saved, but when the flames turned away for good, I felt defeated. If it all had burned, we'd have been free. Holding nothing but a few photographs and a single suitcase, we might have carried on, moving fast, traveling light.

At dusk, the electric whine of cicadas travels in waves through the cedars. One of them, a tiny dragon the size of my thumb, has landed here on a post. Little monster, I know you. I was born to your mad song.

In a turnout off the ridge road, someone left a pair of red, sequined, high-heeled shoes. They'd sharpened two short, thick spikes and driven them through the sole of each shoe into the hardpack. Teenagers sometimes park there to make out or drink beer, and loggers stop to check their loads before descending the grade. I once dragged a dead stag off the road at that spot. The deer was missing an eye, and its tongue had been nearly torn away. I pulled it by the antlers, and tumbled it into the gorge.

The farmhouse with its tiled roof is a sun-struck island. A crane hunts frogs in the flooded field.

In Chiapas, at the entrance to a meditation chamber near the great pyramid of Palenque, my brother showed me the stone carving of a Mayan priest holding a mushroom, then opened a bag filled with mushrooms soaked in honey, and said, help yourself. We followed a wide stream to a waterfall, and I swam to a rock in the middle of a pool below the falling water. A thousand chirping birds sang in a single voice. A butterfly landed on my shoulder, then another, until my body was covered with them. I felt as if I'd blossomed. That morning, a woman in the marketplace had given me a small bird carved out of jade, and said, you will need this. I held the bird before me like a divining rod, and followed it out of the jungle. The sun set, and in the darkness, fireflies tore holes in the night's fabric—bursts of light from the world behind this one. My brother found a car with keys in the ignition, and we drove down a narrow dirt track. We didn't get far. Up ahead, the Serpent God stood on the side of the road. Bright plumes adorned his head and spilled over his shoulders. He wore a cape made of hummingbird feathers, and carried a stone sword that he rested against a belt heavy with human skulls. My brother began to pull the car over, but I turned, and said, don't pick him up.

The porch light throws shadows on the far side of the canyon. The pickets and posts of the railing cast the bars of an enormous cage, and I can see a giant—dark, featureless—pace between the redwoods and the granite cliffs, his terrible head large as a boulder. He fumes and broods, but at last he stops, soothed by the stream flowing over stones that snag the black water and give it voice.

We walked past the jail where a woman shouted to someone waving from the window of his cell. At the corner of 4th and Broadway, a sign on a shuttered bar said, *Goodbye—and thanks to our loyal customers*. Delivery trucks had snapped the lower limbs off the sycamores that lined the street, but the leaves high above rustled in a breeze coming in from the bay. Gene and I stepped into his lobby. An orchid sat on a brushed steel shelf. The elevator opened, closed, and when it opened again, we were at Gene's door. Elizabeth's hat and scarf were still hanging in the hall. That's where she died, where Gene had asked, are you leaving me, and she'd said, yes.

A young woman in wooden shoes and a brilliant, flowered kimono played an amplified, electric koto. When I introduced myself, she saw that I had bought a recording of her music. I knew she was only trying to invite me to her next performance, but I blushed when she threw her arms around me, kissed me hard on the cheek, and said, come to my life!

It's not the breasts or the pose that makes the sculpture so alluring, but the model's willingness to respond to the sculptor's commands, his hand pushing one shoulder forward from the other, the weight of her body held now by a slab of bronze. Slender legs, burnished shoulders—the landscape of a country that men will defend with their lives, and sons will carry their father's bones a thousand miles to bury them there.

Bamboo, heavy with summer rain, bends to reveal a stand of pine trees at the crest of a hill, and just beyond, a single trawler sliding over the bay.

I was looking for a word, but I couldn't find it. I struggled for that word, but it wouldn't come. On a train from Penn Station to Springfield, Massachusetts, I once met a charming, beautiful girl. She mesmerized me, and told me her name, but it's gone now. Everything seems to be slipping away. I once had a friend from Serbia, or Azerbaijan; I can't remember which. Scaffolding, apostrophe, cosseted—I lost these words, but they came back to me. If I lost them for good, how would I know?

In the facility, those who could, spoke, and those who could not, listened. A woman stood to one side. Her face was placid, but it was clear that she wanted to join in. At last there was a pause, and she asked no one in particular, am I dead?

Not yet morning but no longer night, the sky peach-hued at the horizon, cicadas began their chorus, and two crows called out as they flew beneath a half-moon stranded in the wakening sky.

From the vineyard, the comet was just visible above the tree line. No fireball with blazing tail, just a smear of light against the heavens. The stars were brilliant that night, but none were as bright as the comet. Both of my boys were asleep in the car. The comet will not return in my lifetime, or theirs. I wanted them to see it, but it was late, and it wasn't worth disturbing them for that little feathery wisp.

We followed a trail beside a mountain stream, and below us, in the water, tiny trout followed us upstream. As we walked, larger fish joined the others, and when we reached the shrine at the end of the trail, there were a dozen fish large enough to eat milling in a pool. At the shrine, we met a man in uniform, and thought he might turn us away, but when I pointed to the fish gathered in the stream, he lifted a tarp from the back of his pickup, pointed to a fishing rod, and laughed.

The slash pile spits and cracks as the branches burst with the heat of the fire. The sounds are amplified back from the woods, and though I know there's no one there, it's impossible not to hear footsteps, and think someone, or something, is walking in the shadows just beyond reach of the light that jumps and shimmers with the flames.

I followed a path along the cliffs at the water's edge, and a whale swam beside me as I walked. He arched his back and disappeared beneath the surface, then breached and fixed on me. Sardines were shoaling, and he moved through them at my own measured pace, his breath a fine, grey mist. Each time he surfaced, he turned his head and looked at me. A humpback's eye is small for such an enormous body, still, this one's was as large as my fist, and when he submerged, then lunged straight into the air, I could see the black ring around an eye blue as deep water, which caught me in its gaze.

The old scholar explained the significance of the Chinese characters, and their importance to the Buddhist ideal of non-attachment. His baggy pants were gathered by a belt hitched up to its last notch. When I said, I think you exemplify that ideal, he looked at me with his one good eye, shook his head and said, oh no, I am not like that at all. I have desires. I would like some water, he said smiling. I desire water.

A dense fog settled over the mountain. Redwoods, immense in their bulk, vanished into the mist. Deer had torn the lower limbs from the apple tree, and while I bent down to gather them, five vultures fell through the fog and teetered on the air, surprised to find themselves so close to the ground.

All morning a robin flew into the window at the back of my room. He flung himself at his reflection, and beat at it with his wings. He flew away, and returned to attack again and again. In that light, he could see himself clearly.

The blaze spread quickly through the heavy brush, crowned in the pines, and exploded in the redwoods. Flames rose and fell as if the woods were breathing fire. My family was safe, evacuated from the mountain, but I stayed behind to save the house if I could. I sat in the dark and smoked a fat cigar, blew smoke at the smoke that rose from the ruin of the forest. Sparks flew all around. Everything was turning to smoke and snowy ash. I took a breath, and held it.

She stared at the old woman staggering across the street, and said, don't ever let me get like that; put a pillow over my face. She turned to her daughter, and said, oh, you'd never do it. Then her eyes lit up, and she said, your husband might.

We passed a rowboat high in an oak tree, a rat's nest on the hood of an abandoned car; bedsprings, bottles, a porcelain stove. There were chanterelles on the hillside, and on the cliff that dropped into a gorge, and though there was ruin all around us, we gathered them.

Tiny moths appear and vanish, reappear, and vanish a moment later. There must be a shaft of light striking them from above, or the moths have found a way to travel between worlds.

Music marks time—gathers, embraces, and endures it. Thunder in the tympani, nectar in the run of a flute; arpeggios of wonder, terror, and desire. When the orchestra plays, the world flies at us on a fierce wind. Abandoned to the music, you ask yourself— how long have my eyes been closed; how long since I've taken a breath?

A warbling vireo called all night from the cottonwoods above the stream, and in the morning, the air was perfumed with prairie rose. Hummingbirds came and went from the feeder on the porch. Wood lily and dogbane were in blossom beneath the aspens, and mariposa lilies swayed between boulders above the pasture. Their white petals rest on slender stalks that rise from a tuber. Bears dig through the snow for them in winter, and the settlers here survived on them that first terrible winter when their stores ran out.

Here on the mountain, I've gathered bones, spear points, stone scrapers. When the owls call out, I call back. A Grizzly Bear still haunts the place. I keep his teeth in a drawer in my desk—where else would he go? He sends a bobcat to stand watch outside my door, and yesterday a cougar ran in circles by the burn pile. I've lived under these trees for a long time. I may just stay forever.

My son put a sheet of paper in the middle of a field to catch whatever fell from the sky. My son was patient, not afraid to wait. Under a microscope, he identified pollen, dead skin, bits of insect wing, and put a magnet to the rest. He lifted the tiny specks for me to see. He was old enough to know what he was hungry for, and what he'd found. Look, he said, stardust.

We harvested all the persimmons we could reach, and left what remained for the birds. Juncos, warblers and winter wrens buried themselves in the fruit, gorged on the pulp until nothing was left but empty skin, prayer flags stuttering in the wind. Now the birds cry out from the highest branches of the tree, while at the foot of the mountain, children are singing in a bright room, where their friend, a sweet, redheaded boy, is dying.

Deer fern and bracken rise from the scorched earth where last year's fire raged, a green tide lapping at the charred remains of the pines and Manzanita. It's promise and renewal, but in the moonlight, all a ghostly ash.

After the harvest, beside a path overlooking the ocean and worn, mudstone shelves battered by rain, Killarney and my wife gleaned artichokes from their brittle stalks, the leaves burned silver by an early frost. The copper buds on a stand of willows glistened in the swale below, and sea lions called after us as we staggered to the road, our backpacks filled with the monstrous thistles that we'd soon be eating for dinner.

The fire spared our house, turned toward the winery, and bolted down the canyon. Everyone assumed the grapes on the ridge were a loss, but when I open a bottle of Pinot from the vineyard here on Battle Mountain, 2009, the year of the blaze, the scent of ash is on the cork, and I taste the true terroir of home: sun and rain, minerality from the granite soil, and catastrophe. In this vintage, there's dark chocolate and briar in the glass, strawberry and plum in the mouth, and in the finish—smoke.

I fell asleep on a bench at Heart's Desire Beach, and dreamed the vultures that teetered above Tomales Bay were bolts of black cloth spiraling over the water. The day before, at our father's funeral, my brother had draped everything with black lace. Children on the beach squealed and ran through the shallow water holding stingrays by their tails. Lying there still half-asleep, I heard the children's voices rise and fall, and those treacherous fish with their menacing spines fluttered, spun, and were carried away on the wind.

My son is good with numbers. He liked to count the pennies in my pocket. He counted the cars on the highway; forks and spoons, cups and saucers. He assigned them all a number, and kept a tally. I once found him sitting in his room over pages filled with ciphers. He looked at me and said, I want to know how everything adds up.

Because I didn't speak Japanese, they sat me with the children who were talking to a priest. The children asked him questions, and when they laughed, the old man laughed as well. The screens were open to the temple garden on two sides of the hall, and a butterfly, black as the priest's silk robes, flew in and out of view. A trickle of water entered a length of bamboo, which filled and then emptied itself with a hollow chime; was filled and emptied again, so that time was marked by that slow beat. When the priest had finished talking, my friend said, the children were asking him about death, and where children go when they die. The priest told them, if you believe in heaven, you'll go to heaven. If you believe in hell, you'll go to hell. But really, he said, there is no heaven, and no hell, and when children die, they just move from one place to another. The bamboo in the little stream clacked behind us, righted itself, and the water began filling it again.

Our house sits above Mill Creek, which flows to the San Vicente, and empties into the cold Pacific. A small stream flows from a pond just uphill of us, and joins the larger stream below. It's too small to have a name, but we could call it Granite Falls, or Wild Iris, Steep Water or Little Spring. I like Four Souls Creek. I'll have to think about it. The name should be beautiful; the stream encircles us, and this is the water that we drink.

ACKNOWLEDGMENTS

Grateful acknowledgment is made to the following magazines where many of these poems previously appeared:

The American Journal of Poetry: "On Sunday afternoons"

Askew: "The slash pile spits and cracks," "Beach grass caught the milky froth"

Catamaran: "It was five o'clock," "The fire grew larger every day"

Chicago Quarterly Review: "In a shack outside Oaxaca," "We grew up hearing war stories," "All morning a robin"

Cloudbank: "As a guide described the origins," "The whale's tooth, "My son was good with numbers"

Denver Quarterly: "All that's left"

45th Parallel: "Repeated beneath the surface of the pond," "At dusk, a whale surfaced," "In a turnout off the ridge road"

Hotel Amerika: "Not yet morning," "Bamboo, heavy with summer," "14,000 years ago," "The farmhouse with its tiled roof," "We climbed the mountain"

Miramar: "At sixty," "Driving from the valley," "Because I didn't speak Japanese"

The New Flash Fiction Review: "In the facility," "The porch light throws shadows," "We walked past the jail"

The Packinghouse Review: "At dusk, the whine of cicadas," "As usual, the birds wake me," "We followed a trail beside a mountain stream"

Ploughshares: "In the woods, hunting mushrooms," "Five ravens climbed a redwood"

phren-Z: "Deer fern and bracken rise," "One day past the solstice," "She stared at the old woman," "Tiny moths appear and vanish"

Quarter After Eight: "I can't remember everything," "Here on the mountain"

Red Wheelbarrow: "After the harvest," "Music marks time"

The Rumpus: "A young woman in wooden shoes," "The old scholar explained"

Spillway: "Gathering mushrooms in the forest," "My son put a piece of paper"

StringTown: "The boy rode his bike," "We harvested the persimmons"

Many of these poems appeared in *Adversary,* published in Miramar Editions' chapbook series. Others were published in a limited edition artist's book from Ninja Press, *In Japan.* Several of these poems appeared in *California Prose Directory 2017: New Writing from the Golden State,* Outpost 19 Books. "It was five o'clock" appeared in *First Light: A Festschrift for Philip Levine on his 85th Birthday,* the Press at Fresno State University/Greenhouse Review Press. "Because I didn't speak Japanese" was awarded the Lucille Medwick Memorial Award from the Poetry Society of America. "We grew up hearing war stories," "I can't remember everything," "The boy rode his bike," "The whale tooth was etched," and "Driving from the valley" were awarded the George Bogin Memorial Award from the Poetry Society of America. Several of these poems were written while serving as Poet-in-Residence at the Cabrillo Festival of Contemporary Music.

"Fives ravens climbed a redwood" is for Stephen Kessler
"It was five o'clock" is for Paula Falconer and Angelo Benvenuto
"At sixty" is for Christopher Buckley
"It's not the breasts" is for Manuel Neri
"The old scholar" is for Dr. Noritoshi Aramaki
"Music marks time" is for Marin Alsop
"A warbling vireo" is for Margi Schroth
"We harvested all the persimmons" is for Connor Cockerham

Special thanks to Christopher Buckley, Killarney Clary, and Brad Crenshaw

ABOUT THE AUTHOR

Gary Young is a poet, artist, and translator. He is author of eight collections of poetry, among them *Even So: New and Selected Poems*; limited edition letterpress books; and numerous chapbooks. His poems have appeared in over one hundred anthologies. He co-edited the critical anthologies *One for the Money: The Sentence as a Poetic Form*, *Bear Flag Republic: Prose Poems and Poetics from California*, and *The Geography of Home: California's Poetry of Place*. His many honors include the Shelley Memorial Award and the William Carlos Williams Award, both from the Poetry Society of America. He has received grants from the National Endowment for the Humanities, two fellowship grants from the National Endowment for the Arts, the California Arts Council, and the Vogelstein Foundation, among others. He has also received a Pushcart Prize, the Peregrine Smith Poetry Prize, the James D. Phelan Award, and various fellowships and residencies. His print work is represented in collections including the Museum of Modern Art, the Victoria and Albert Museum, and The Getty Center for the Arts. He teaches creative writing and directs the Cowell Press at the University of California, Santa Cruz.